The Journey to Here

Joanne Baker

The Journey to Here

The Journey to Here
ISBN 978 1 74027 808 9
Copyright © text Joanne Baker 2013
Cover image: Garry Swyghuizen

First published 2013
Reprinted 2015

Ginninderra Press
PO Box 3461 Port Adelaide SA 5015
www.ginninderrapress.com.au

Contents

Darkness or Light	7
Dark 1988–1993	**9**
Friends	11
Final Death	13
Entrapment	14
The Hunt	15
Is There Meaning?	16
For Johnnie Boy	17
Without Love	18
Even In My Arms You're Out of Reach	19
Lord of the Plain	20
Help Me	21
Empathy	22
How I Wish	24
I Am You	25
It Happens (with a 'sh')	26
Cocooned	27
Eternity	29
Confessions to the Mirror	30
The Innocent's Pain	31
The Owl and the Bird	32
Keep Dreaming	34
Grey 2006–2007	**37**
Classified	39
The Task	41
Brother	42
What am I?	43
Angel	44
For Rhiannon	46
Venting	47

Happily Burning Bridges	48
The World Turns	49
I Will Tell You Why	50
A Result of Your Apathy	51
Don't Lose Your Temper	52
Can You Meet Me?	53
Poisoned Black Fingerprint	54
Your Heart's Not in Your Eyes	55
Light 2010–2012	**57**
The Billabong's Silent Scream	59
When I Saw the Light 1	61
When I Saw the Light 2	62
A 'Creative' Mills & Boon	63
By a Whisker	65
Saving Worms	67
The House at the End of the Street	69
S's Sweet Seduction	70
A Very Strange Person	71
Colour	72
One Day in June	73
There's No Time	74
The Dance	75
Web Attack	76
Inspiration	77
Hair	78
Love	80
The Cat in the Window	81
Why Would You Do That?	83
Crush	84
The Route to the Rout	85
The Tale of an Old Pair of Boots	87

Darkness or Light

I once walked in darkness and what could I see?
It was a misshapen echo, a doppelganger of me.
She would carelessly cut me then leave me to bleed;
I must head to the light so I won't drown in need.

When I walk in the light, well, what can I say?
There's another echo that won't turn away.
I'm enfolded with love and maternal praise
And the words that I write I like to see on a page.

When I walked in the darkness, the words that I wrote,
While sometimes were beautiful, were lacking in hope.
It's the path that I walked just so I could cope
But the dark of the path was limited in scope.

So I'll walk in the light for as long as I know
That the way to the light is to let darkness go
And fertiliser happens so good stuff can grow
And the seed to my happiness only I can sow.

Dark 1988–1993

Friends

I think of all the friends I've known
Who I've trusted with my life
Who've only turned around
And stabbed me with a knife.

They've destroyed my self-esteem
And ripped apart my will
Yet when they want my friendship back
I'm there and trusting still.

I should have learnt by now
I should have learnt to hate
But trust is all I've ever known
And I always trust a mate.

They talk behind my back
And make a fool of me
Yet I won't listen to the truth
And I'm too blind to see.

When I'm on a high
They are there as well
But when I lose, or when I'm down
Then I can go to hell.

I should be less trusting
Is what my true friends say
Yet when it comes to friendship
I can't tell night from day.

Maybe if I had less heart
And didn't pick up strays
Then maybe I could pick my friends
And wouldn't hurt this way.

Friends should be there always
Through the thick and thin
I dedicate to all my mates
And those who've never been.

Final Death

When dreams will turn to nightmares
And daytime turns to dark
The magnificent to ugly
And the beautiful to stark.

This will be our ending
There will be no more
Our world's worst catastrophe
The end, a nuclear war.

There may be some survivors
But they won't live for long
Their triumphs all forgotten
No words to give a song.

The innocent will suffer
For no one can we save
Our earth will be infertile
Just one gigantic grave.

Entrapment

Here I walk upon a bed of thorns.
Nothing can hurt me for pain I have scorned
And nothing can stop me for, oh, can't you see?
Pain is nothing and nothing is me.

I've trained myself so not to care
For love is wonderful but life is not fair
You can love with all heart but there's no guarantee
You can be chained; I'd rather be free.

No one will hold me for I show contempt
In this fight that I hold no quarter is lent
I fight with the world and my worst enemy
My fight is hopeless for I'm fighting with me.

So no matter who wins I'm the loser as well
Building the walls to my own private hell
Through the bars I have built the sky I can see
There's the world all around but I'll never be free.

The Hunt

The pounding of the darkness
The rhythm of the night
The cruelty of the hateful dreams
The uselessness of flight.

The emotions of the hunters
Their cold, unholy glee
The taste of blood upon their lips
Their thrill near ecstasy.

The victim runs with terror
His pulse so close to mine
He can't avoid the hunter's eyes
No escape is there to find.

No alleyways to turn down
No hole in which to hide
With weariness upon his heart
He turns prepared to die.

No hate upon his handsome face
No wavering of his gaze
He loses life not dignity
In a metal-blinded haze.

The hunters crowd around the corpse
To them a fruitful day
They leave a god upon the sand
To rot and waste away.

Is There Meaning?

Murderers they still escape
Dangerous men are left to rape
Our wondrous world is full of hate
And what's its meaning?

There's no punishment to fit the crime
No way to clean us of this grime
The result is quick, we have no time
To find out its true meaning.

Murderers still walk the street
The police are afraid to walk their beat
All are scared, psychotic heat
And we know there is no meaning.

What we need is hope it seems
Enough to fill the world with dreams
We'll try to work out what it means
'Cause all our world has lost its soul
Is hope enough to make us whole?

For Johnnie Boy

What was that, that breath of air?
If I turn around, will you be there?
My mind, I know, will see the fact
You're gone forever, you can't come back.

I remember how we played the game
We broke the rules, it was all the same
'Cause rules are fine for the privileged some
You cheated bad; still the bastards won.

Life was hard enough on you
You had the worst yet you'd pulled through
You lived the bad where most can't cope
Your life ahead was full of hope.

Then came the night when you were pissed
They took their shot, they didn't miss
A car was driven, a twist of fate
You were walking home; we'll miss you, mate.

Without Love

I see you gaze and you close your eyes
I see your pain but you do not cry
I see you hope but it is never
For without love we have forever.

Your love I want but you do not see
Our love can only shackle me
For all our longing to be together
Without love we have forever.

Can't you see I need you, friend?
But with love this thing will end
And your friendship's something that I treasure
And I promise you I want forever.

Even In My Arms You're Out of Reach

Your looks so perfect, your eyes so true
Your heart an enigma, am I nothing to you?
Your attitude temperate, you're slow to enrage
You gather up people to display in your cage.

I'm under your power, you know I won't fight
But you treat me different and somehow that's right
You treat me as equal, a secret we share
I defend you as holy; you know I'll be there.

Would you treat me as equal if you knew of my dream?
Of loving you fully, of reigning supreme
Of hearing you call out my name in your sleep
Of giving your heart up to me just to keep.

Would it matter to you if you felt the same?
Would you go with the impulse or hide out in shame?
Would you ever forgive me for showing I care?
But I love you so badly you know I won't dare.

I cannot risk something so right and so real
By telling you of things that you mightn't feel
By telling the truth the result would be clear
It would be all or nothing and it's nothing I fear.

So I will be comfort when you are in pain
I'll continue my dreaming and pretend I'm the same
'Why can't you love me?' to the moon I will preach
I can tell by your eyes that you're still out of reach.

Lord of the Plain

I breathe the wind; it makes me fly
I stamp the ground; I cannot die
No man's heels have touched my flank
And in my freedom my gods I thank.

Through restless worlds where angels lie
Eagles soar from behind my eye
I am the spirit; I'm always free
No man on earth can conquer me.

I am the spirit; the restless wind
I am the spirit; I am the end
I'll not be seen before you die
I am the earth; I am the sky.

With my mane of rippling silk
I feed on sun, my mother's milk
And from my loins spring forth the plain
I am the hunter; I am the game.

I am the spirit no one can tell
The air you breathe my lungs expel
I am the spirit; your soul is mine
I rear and wheel; the lord of time.

Help Me

The wind it cuts through all that's shown
And I look up; no wind has blown
Within me seeds of doubt are sown
So I run for all my life.

There's no escaping that restless wind
It follows me towards soul's end
It cuts strength down, my only friend
Alone: it sees my life.

It asks me words; I cannot lie
One false move and I know I'll die
For all my wrongs I don't know why
I'll fight for all my life.

Help me – yes, I want to live
Help me now, my soul I give
Help me now my truth must hide
To see my truth is suicide.

Empathy

Your pain as harsh as it can be
I see you flinch with empathy
You feel your sorrow will never pass
Take every breath as if your last.

What you feel I know inside
The heart that breaks, the loss of pride
The trust that's gone, the false belief
The thought of only death's release.

The smile you show is a lie on your face
'Cause friendship is nothing that hate can't erase
And friendship may cause you to live once again
And living's unknown, you're familiar with pain.

When? Can't you tell me when?
The past has died, please live again
You need my help, I'll be there, friend
I'll help you stand while our world may end
(But you know that I'll be there.)

I try so hard to see your mind
Inside your head, hurt's all I find
Jammed full of hate you think you earn
I see the chaos, I feel it burn.

You suffer in silence, won't let out your rage
Forging the bars of your internal cage
Hoarding up horrors to fester within
For maybe in death your real life begins.

Why? Can't you tell me why?
Jump off the edge, to soar you try
A life so new, you live to die
I love you true, you think I lie
How can I prove I care?
I will be there
When the odds are too great
Then call on me, mate
And together our fate we will share
For whatever will be, through eternity
If you need someone, I will be there.

How I Wish

I feel so used, so torn apart
The battles over, one broken heart
You know how I feel, my heart it will heal
And I know how you cannot be near
And it's you that I need, while our broken hearts bleed
Oh God, how I wish you were here.

A shoulder to cry on is what you have been
A person to care for, my soul you have seen
You know me so well, together lived hell
You taught me to love, not to fear
And it seems like forever since we were together
But God, how I wish you were here.

Do you feel the same as me?
The love is gone, before it could be
And where your heart was, a hole does remain
And remembering pleasure brings back the pain.

If you were here, I could help you through
But it is a wish and that just will not do
But remember our past and your smile it will last
And remember I promise I care
If I wasn't tied down, well then, I'd be around
Oh God, how I wish I was there.

Oh, the fun that we shared
The hearts that we bared
We would laugh while the others would sneer
You taught me to care, to live life a dare
Oh God, how I wish you were here.

I Am You

You feel the sun burn on your back
There's nothing left, still you attack
You've taken from you all your best
So now the persecution rests.

Why you do this no one knows
But still you let this hatred grow
You don't try hard, so you only see
Your back to walls, you're facing me.

Face to face and eyes to eyes,
I'm all the things that you despise
I am the truth, the worst of lies
Accept me, I am you.

I am you, what else is true?
Accept the love you never knew
Accept the hope or we're both through
Accept me, I am you.

I am you, how could this be?
You look for truth you'll never see
I am your eyes, come see through me
And love me, I am you.

All idle comments lost in doubt
Hidden meanings you can't work out
I am your ears, I hear you shout
I'll help you…for I am you.

It Happens (with a 'sh')

All the time it happens
Every part in every day
Don't you know it happens?
There could be no other way.

Can't you see it happens?
It won't let you reach your goal
And as it will, it happens
Circumstance beyond control.

But even though it happens
You can smile and still aim high
'Cause as it is, it happens
If you didn't laugh you'd cry.

So while you know it happens
Situations soon reverse
So remember while it happens
Things could be a damn sight worse.

Cocooned

I watched you shrink within your shell
With hopeless odds you've fought like hell
Though wounded bad you're still not beat
If you're to win you must retreat.

Weave a web around your soul
They can't get in, you can grow whole
Find strength within, you know it's there
You'll change the odds, you'll make it fair.

I see you grow in your cocoon
Use your strength, don't seal your tomb
As you emerge your beauty's shown
Go show the world, I've always known.

Your wings unfurl, though they're still wet
You must escape the 'normal' net
The ones that tie you down with tears
Who hate you with unfounded fears.

Beware of ones that act with class
They'll pin you down, display in glass
So all their friends can look and see
Just what a rebel they can be.

And you will wither, shrink and die
You grew your wings, you'll never fly
Is this the life, the fate you choose?
You have the choice, you can refuse.

You can pick the ones to trust
Choose them wisely, you know you must
To see their souls you read their eyes
The ones that touch you teach to fly.

Your choice is there as you can see
You can refute normality
In what you choose your fate will pass
Please don't get trapped beneath the glass.

Eternity

I see you cry; are your tears for me?
Do you say goodbye? For eternity?
Do you remember dreams? The future we shared?
Do you remember the screams? The hearts that we bared?

Do you remember with hate, the things we once had?
Do you forget all the great and replace it with bad?
Remember the good, for all else is pale
Remember we could, forget that we fail.

I never even said goodbye
Is it for you or me you cry?
I said forever I'd be there
Remember me for I still care.

You cannot feel me, we cannot touch
Your life and mine, was it too much?
The gods insulted, I don't know how
I said forever, forever's now.

And so it's over, no final breath
The words 'I love you' fall to death
My tears are frozen, though I die
It's not for me but for you I cry.

Confessions to the Mirror

All control I've held on me
All truth is never seen
There's nothing that I've told to you
No goodness has there been.

I know myself for what I am
And I lie to cover facts
I fight to hide the past from view
But the past keeps coming back.

I won't tell you of my crimes of old
But even I, I must confess
To extract this poison from my soul
To get this hatred off my chest.

So I confess into the mirror
I tell all the truth I can
I smash the image that I show
And I see me as I am.

The lies are stripped away from me
When I look into the glass
The fancy future that I show
Is replaced by truths of past.

Only I made all my past that way
Only I hate having lied
Only I am what I am today
Don't you think I'm satisfied?

Only I will tell the truth to me
Only I get justice done
Only I know my depravity
Only I, I am the one.

The Innocent's Pain

When a child is abused we don't know of the cost
We don't know of the pain or the innocence lost
We don't know the betrayal or how it could feel
We don't know the hurt or the guilt that seems real.

We know something's changed but we do not know why
When faced with the truth we'd much rather the lie
The parent won't see it and the child can't say
So we bury our heads and hope it all goes away.

And the heartless abuser hopes the kid will forget
So that person won't think of their own cheap regret
'It's only a child so their memory's not long',
They don't think of the loss, of the life that's gone wrong.

And what of the child, of the face we don't see?
Of the happier times there is no memory
It's all overshadowed by the guilt and the shame
And if life goes on, it is never the same.

The Owl and the Bird

The wise owl said to the little bird
I don't care what you've seen or heard
Or what you've lived or who you be
I am the wisest listen to me.

I've seen it all, I hold the truth
I know your world, you don't need proof
All your life I've lived you know
Listen to what I say or go.

But the bird questioned the wise old owl
To live your life, I don't know how
How can you know my own life's trial?
Is what I've lived so gross, so vile?

How can you know of how I live?
Of the parts of me I've had to give?
Of what I've seen and had to fight?
How can you know, you live in night?

Have you seen rain, have you seen sun?
Have you tried freedom just for fun?
Have you seen the colours of the flower?
You can't have lived my greatest hour.

You can't have lived my greatest fears
If you had you'd know my tears
You'd know my tears have made me strong
So what you've told me must be wrong.

How can you know what gives me pain?
After every step of what I'll gain
After every fall I know I'll rise
Is to see me fall what you despise?

Is it to see me rise and then succeed?
To see me smile even though I bleed
To see me learn even while I grow
To change the things you think you know.

Do you hate to think that you could learn
From a way of life I know you spurn
'Cause everything's not cut and dried
When you see the world through other's eyes.

Keep Dreaming

The load is slowly lifted
The ground it slowly shifts
Where once there was an uphill track
A downhill can exist.

There's no need to struggle down that road
You can stroll and look at life
You can choose your turnings, choose your load
Each day will then suffice.

Or you can exist the way you are
Conversing to yourself
Thinking of those grandiose dreams
And hoping there's no help.

You keep thinking there's no chances
That only, if, you could
You'd be a heroine of old
But if you could, you would.

Do you believe the things you say?
Do those grandiose dreams still melt away?
Do you look at life and live the day?
If you think you do, you're dreaming.

Did you think that they could never see?
You liked the guilt, the misery
You lived for it; it was all you'd be
So now you change, keep dreaming.

I'm not trying to discourage you
For all your dreams you never knew
You were taught your place, where nothing grew
So now you've moved, keep dreaming.

You can turn, you can try
Your arms are pinions, you can fly
And when you're higher it may be seen
There's nothing wrong; you're right to dream.

Grey 2006–2007

Classified

Yes, I wear my hair real short
And look suave in men's gear
But I am still a woman so
I write this to make things clear.

I'm young and free and meant to be
I believe in fate, in destiny
I believe in love with no regrets
I believe in peace, in happiness.

I believe in truth, no need to lie
The life I live I won't deny
I believe in hope and strength through pain
I believe that life repeats again.

Déjà vu to me's a sign
To tell you that your life's on line
That soon there'll be a lesson learnt
Same time in life, this time not burnt.

I believe in loyalty and friends
I believe we all will meet again
I believe we all must pay our way
If not this life some other day.

I believe that yin and yang is true
No right or wrong but a different view
And there is reason in every fall
And the strength to be weak makes a person stand tall.

So in what hole should I be classed?
The poet, the friend, the piece of ass
The dyke, the dreamer, the person that cries
The person that laughs and will no more despise?

I am me and you are you
And variety is life it's true
There's no one else I'd rather be
And my words are just a part of me.

The Task

You hear the rhythm pounding
As you're looking all around
The drums are from beneath you
Your extension to the ground
You know the task that lies ahead
But excitement builds the same
The line between master and team
An intoxicating game.

You communicate your tension
To the body you know well
You feel that he's responding
And you know that he can tell
He knows now what it is you want
And the sweat begins to rise
The ground is not the one he knows
But the task is no surprise.

Brother

Golden child, chosen one
First and only favoured son
You cannot face your fear, I see
But I can't see why you're scared of me.

Six-foot-four, strong and proud
Can you even say my name out loud?
The one man that I looked up to
What has ten years done to you?

What resentments are unsaid?
Did you ever truly wish me dead?
Remember once comrades in arms
Did you ever really wish me harm?

Remember we were underdogs
A lot of times we beat the odds
The proudest moments that I had
Involved a horse truck, you and Dad.

It's why we fought both tooth and nail
We were reaching for the holy grail
Because we both fought for the prize
One had to be cut down to size.

So when one won, we both were lost
Our peace perhaps became the cost
We're not competing now at all
And I am neither strong nor tall.

I have one thing, I have my pride
For you I'll put that one aside
It's no small thing to me, it's true
But is all I have enough for you?

What am I?

On padded feet I haunt the night
Waiting for when the moment's right
To take the prey by complete surprise
And taste the moment as it dies.

To feel my fangs sink in its neck
To stop its pulse with no regret
I let it go and then give chase
'Cause fear gives meat that tangy taste.

I see you wince and hear you moan
But I know you, I'm not alone
I know you all have friends like me
Who find joy in others' misery.

Whether they are kin or not
They're more alive when the blood is hot
'Cause when the moment is just right
We all are creatures of the night.

Angel

You called me an angel but that's not my name
You gave me ideals that I could not attain
I tell you I'm human but you won't heed my call
You kept calling me angel but angels do fall.

You thought me an angel or said I was one
But I think that that's flying too close to the sun
If I flew up there my wings would be burned
But the heat was so sweet and so I never learned.

I strived so hard to be the saviour you sought
But I am no Jesus and salvation's not bought
I wanted to give you the moon and the sky
But you didn't need it you were already high.

You were there flying before I was around
The first time I met you your feet touched the ground
I feel like I trapped you when you wanted to stay
How could we have realised the price we'd both pay?

While I was there floating on an emotional breeze
I felt your longing and responded with greed
For the first time you felt your emotions were real
But you think they're too much for one person to feel.

Like a kite made of silver on a gossamer thread
The wind broke your chains and it left you for dead
You needed my weight there to anchor you down
But the water has risen and I'm starting to drown.

You need to be soaring with those of your kind
Not down here with me and my cynical mind
I won't cut you loose like they have done before
But I'll give you my rope then I'll make you some more.

For though I have loved you a part of you dies
When you fly down from those hot summer skies
But your wings have regrown and now you're free
To become the angel you said I could be.

For Rhiannon

Hubble, bubble, toil and trouble
For you, my dear, there is no double
My shining light, my dream come true
My one and only, baby, you.

Your smile lights like sweet sunshine
I'm proud a part of you is mine
And every moment seems so sweet
With you I feel my life's complete.

I'm mostly happy when you're around
Your laughter makes the sweetest sound
It barrels up from within your chest
I don't need no more, I have the best.

And yes you are the best to me
No matter what your destiny
You'll always be my chosen one
I'm glad it's you that calls me Mum.

Venting

I say that I am handling it, that I've been doing well
But that is such a goddamn lie, I've been through living hell.

I'm smoking like a chimney, bit my fingers till they bled
But I thought I finally got it, finally got you from my head.

Then you crooked a finger and I followed at your call
I did exactly what you said, it made me feel so small.

You smiled that special smile of yours and yanked upon my lead
I knew just what you wanted then, satisfaction guaranteed.

And as was ordered I did deliver
That moaning, shaking, endless shiver
You called my name at the final high
And I held you, and I felt you cry.

You know how much, to me, it meant
But it didn't matter, you were spent
You went to sleep and gave me time
To think my thoughts and write my rhyme.

I've never been this angry, I've gotten so damn mad
I don't care about the future or the history that we've had.

I don't care about the words you say, they've all been said before
So when you want your cheapest thrill, go somewhere else to score.

Happily Burning Bridges

I found out you were lying
You were doing it to me
But I handled it in my own time
Now it's time to set you free.

I thought you were the only one
A partner made to size
Someone I'd live and die for
But babe I just got wise.

I've cooked your meals for a hundred years
I've taken crap with silent tears
I felt so low, too weak to fight
And I was scum, you're always right.

A loveless scene you know it's true
Infertile ground yet something grew
You could not fight it, for it's inside
And now, alone, I stand in pride.

And there's no way I'd take you back
It's over now so face the fact
Get out of my life, my house, my face
You're just my past so take your place.

The World Turns

Though lust is easy life is not
Sometimes I wish this world would stop
For just one second so I could savour
The sweetness of silence's flavour.

Alone at night when the world's asleep
When the moon hangs low and dreams are deep
When nothing moves, not a breath of air
You can almost feel that second's there.

It's just a moment, an almost blink
There's just no time to even think
That this is it, before it's gone
And once again the world moves on.

I Will Tell You Why

You don't know why I'm angry, please take a second's pause
I'm sure that if you think a bit, you'll see that I have cause.
Still don't know why I'm angry? Please give another try
And then if you can't work it out, then I will tell you why.

Just try and cast your mind back, even for half a year
Can't you see the rage I have is directly due to fear?
Do I have to shout them out, to call them to the sky?
'Cause you don't want to see them, all the reasons why.

You want to know the reason, why our love became a cage?
Here's one of many reasons, your internal burning rage.
I don't know exactly when it was, my fear turned to frustration
But I know now that it meant to me my final liberation.

A Result of Your Apathy

You say that you won't hurt her or ever let her cry
But still you're somehow willing to let her watch you die.
You're wasting down to nothing and if you're seen you're never there
You're just too fucking self-involved to ever really care.

For anything.

You tell me that you love her yet still you let her down
You seem to only say your words just to hear the sound
You pleaded for her presence, that I not take her away
Then after all your teary words, you sent her down the bay.

Alone. With strangers.

How could you ever possibly justify that in your mind?
How can you act so wounded when my reply is then unkind?
You tell all that will listen about how bad your life's become
You refuse to ever really see that you reap what you have done.

Don't Lose Your Temper

You throw your hands up in the air
And almost indulge in great despair
They're erecting roadblocks that still burn
To try to stop your life's return.

They want you to reply in rage
So they can say at any stage
Look at this note she sent to me
Her temper's not controlled you see.

Will lashing out still satisfy?
When you give truth unto their lie?
Swallow those curses they try to entice
Pretend there's no problem and try to be nice.

Use all of your graces and draw on your skill
Have the utmost of patience; the truth is there still
Don't lose your temper, even though it's drawn out
Give them no reason for logical doubt.

Can You Meet Me?

I feel I'm doing everything that I can try to do
To bridge this space between us, so I can share in you
I've given to you openly, my joy, my tears, my shame
You tell me that you love me, but I don't think you feel the same.

I know what stirs inside of me, the emotions that I feel
But is it only in my head, is any of it real?
I want to just believe in us, to love and live in hope
But I fear we're speeding senselessly down a steep and slippery slope.

You seem to think I'm clinging to a thought that's never been
How can we have a future in a past we've never seen?
Back then was just a memory but we must live for now
Or are you so used to looking back you can't remember how?

Can you handle my emotions, the ones that I don't show?
I cannot always voice them so how can you really know?
Your silence speaks in volumes of the fears you cannot say
Would it make it any easier if I quietly went away?

I don't want to seem emotional, it's the person that I am
And if I seem invincible it's because I say I can
It's true that I believe it, though I'd never share my doubt
The illusion of my grandeur is what keeps things working out.

So can you meet me halfway, on a safe and neutral ground?
Can you share with me a love that's free and rarely ever found?
I fear that's not an option as you have drunk away your soul
And no matter what I give of me, I cannot make you whole.

Poisoned Black Fingerprint

I think what you did was so goddamned unfair
'Cause how can a stranger ever compare?
You selfishly left an indelible mark
A poisoned black fingerprint deep in their hearts.

I heard all their words but could not understand
To me what you did was just too coolly planned
You got what you wanted, you opt out at best
And left a poisoned black fingerprint tattooed in flesh.

And I think that it's that that is making me sick
You're the excuse that they use so they can all act like dicks
You took your own life so they'll get stoned or blind
A poisoned black fingerprint deep in their minds.

Your Heart's Not in Your Eyes

I've been waiting patiently
For longing looks I never see
For love to last eternally
But your heart's not in your eyes.

There's tolerance and affection there
And I'm not saying you don't care
But the love I need you do not share
For your heart's not in your eyes.

I feel as though you disapprove
Of an errant child who's sometimes crude
That I'm inadequate in your point of view
And I can't bear that in your eyes.

For I need to feel like I belong
Like all I do is not all wrong
That I'm not weak but sound and strong
But I don't see that in your eyes.

I see a wound that bleeds too deep
A half-led life that's half asleep
Somehow somewhere the angels weep
For your heart's not in your eyes.

Light 2010–2012

The Billabong's Silent Scream

Inspired by *Kings In Grass Castles*

The billabong was calling
Its muted, muffled warning
But no one from the station even stirred
Four families had been mustered
'Cause a black tribe had been busted
Trying to spear some cattle from their herd.

As the men folk rode on by
They could almost hear the sigh
Of the billabong as it tried to find its voice
To the wild life it was screaming
But the warning had no meaning
But it didn't stop, it never had a choice.

They had tracked the black man's tribe
Down to the billabong's side
To where they all had camped the night before
But the tribe had heard the sound
And so no trace could be found
Though the trackers had to stop and look for more.

It was while they all were hunting
That they finally heard something
But by then it was too late to flee the flood
For the river's dam had broken
The billabong had finally spoken
In an avalanche of dirt and rocks and blood.

Four families lost their men
The tribe not seen again
The price of cheap revenge was quite obscene
With the women left alone
Children fatherless at home
'Cause they'd not heard the billabong's silent scream.

When I Saw the Light 1

When I first saw the light
Its glow was clean and bright
It held out against the night
And I knew I must head there.

The light seemed like a beacon
To the truth that I was seekin'
What secret was it keepin'?
I'd find out when I got there.

So I lengthened my stride
Muscles straining under hide
What would the light confide?
I'd find out when I got there.

The light became quite stunning
Like a raging river running
And I a fox with all my cunning
Could only stop and stare.

It only hurt a bit
When the road train finally hit
And in the darkness ended it –
Trapped in the headlights' glare.

When I Saw the Light 2

When I saw the light I never saw its source
When I saw the light I never knew its course
As I saw the light my whole life seemed to fit
For though the light was blinding
I was finding,
I was part of it.

So I knew more than I wanted to
I felt the urge to more than see it through
I understood so therefore I belonged
Yet it seemed to be a siren's song.

But I felt more than I needed to
So I knew more than I ever knew
The light I saw so I belonged
So I gave into the siren's song.

And I knew then as I felt the light
All the truths, all the wrongs from right
But as the truth fades to the afterglow
I've forgotten more than I will ever know.

A 'Creative' Mills & Boon

This is a Mills and Boon type story
A tale of lust and full of glory
Of longing eyes and temperate attitude
Where the men are never dirty
Girls are meek and often flirty
And all are quite aghast when someone's rude.

Enter to our right
Our dashing urban knight
Close by to him a maiden took his eye
She nearly took his life as well
When she beat him half way into hell
The poor bastard was just lucky not to die.

Oh, um… Let me change the scene
Picture every schoolgirl's dream
A knight on his white horse, they're in the sun
He gallops to his maiden
But the poor boy's overladen
And she's trampled when she has no chance to run.

Perhaps I'll try another match
Let's try the 'perfect playboy catch'
He matches with the girl, who's on the rise
That she does her personal trainer
Is truly a no-brainer
When we know he does the chauffeur on the side.

Oh dear, I've done it once again
I fear romance is not my friend
You see, I haven't read a Mills & Boon in years
You know I have my reasons
I could blame it on the seasons
But the truth is that they bore me close to tears.

By a Whisker

By a whisker was his calling card
'By a whisker' he would cry
He lived life by a whisker
And by a whisker he would die.

He snuck in by a whisker
When he had a firm deadline
And often when he broke the law
He got off with a fine.

He got in by just a whisker
When he was running in from hail
And while he succeeded by a whisker
Also sometimes he would fail.

He missed out by just a whisker
When he placed a lotto sum
He got every single number
Only all were out by one.

He won a prize by just a whisker
It was an African safari trip
And he thought the perfect souvenir
Would be a lion's tail tip.

They tried to talk him out of it
But by a whisker he won through
The dumbest form of suicide
There was nothing they could do.

He snuck up on a sleeping lion
And yanked hard upon that fur
And while the man ran very fast
The lion was a blur.

He almost made it to the car
But by a whisker he was caught
And all of his philanthropy
Added up to naught.

So the moral of this story is
When life is getting stale
Don't live it by a whisker
Because dead men pull no tails.

Saving Worms

Do you know that I will try to save
A worm that's drowning in its grave?
To that poor soul I'm God and Lord
And it is saved on a random pause.

Because I looked down and saw it dying
I heard no prayers nor saw it crying
But because I saw it's struggle fade
I raised it up, the choice now made.

So now I have to wonder:
Will it raise its progeny
To believe in me unquestioned
Even till eternity?

Will they worship at the angle
At which I blocked the sun?
Will they build up great worm temples
To which wanted bad worms run?

Will they try to write worm poetry?
Perhaps create worm art?
And with this sense of consciousness
Maybe they'll be quite smart?

And then they'll start to question
The wonders others saw
They'll start to fight amongst themselves,
Perhaps begin a war.

They'll develop separate factions
Say that one side worshipped wrong
Will they mimic our humanity
And create a nuclear bomb?

All these thoughts pass though my head
As I stoop to give my help
It makes me have to wonder
Were we once worms to something else?

The House at the End of the Street

At the house at the end of the street
Even though the lawns were neat
There was something incomplete
And it fascinated me.

I use to peek from behind my curtain
In teenage angst, my life uncertain
I felt its pain, I knew its hurtin'
And it captivated me.

It was almost like it was in my mind
It spoke of owners so unkind
Of ancient hurts and ties that bind
And it tried to make me see.

It said it was a withering shell
White ant infested, salt damp as well
That each day was a living hell
It nearly persuaded me.

It wanted me to end its pain
To burn it down, to rise again
In something better, not the same
I must make my lawyer see.

It was not about development
Or that I spent more than I earnt
In truth it was an accidernt
Perhaps I'll take a plea.

S's Sweet Seduction

You can't see me… Am I even here?
Do come a little closer dear
One step more, you're almost there
It's a food source that's beyond compare.

That's the way, a little more
Have you noticed yet the sweet odour?
There it is; your nose goes up
Come to me, my sweet young pup.

You're almost here, I never shake
Yet still I see you hesitate
Temptingly I wave my lure
You move again, your step unsure.

SNAP!

My arms go out, the sweet embrace
Your touch, your smell, your hot blood taste
I've waited so damned long for you
It's a pity you can't love me too.

My poison pumps, you liquefy
I hold you close as I suck you dry
Ahh…you, my dear, are a tasty brew
A romantic meal; dinner for two.

A Very Strange Person

The circus was here, my excuse to be queer
So just as the day started to fade
My family group, like some big monkey troop
Went to watch at their coming parade.

There were lions and more, even clowns by the score
Even acrobats rolling about
There were strange bearded ladies and all kinds of crazies
And a strongman who had too much clout.

There was a very strange person; of that much I'm certain
I could tell from a cursory glance
They dressed a strange way, yet had nothing to say
But their walk, well it was almost a dance.

They had nearly danced by, when their eye caught on mine
And a knowing smile passed to their lips
They held out a hand and against my command
I reached out for those soft fingertips.

Their laughter was loud; it turned heads in the crowd
I thought it was inebriation
But I could smell their breath; I swear hand to my chest
It must have been sheer jubilation.

But I got drunk on that air, it washed away care
And I laughed with the purest of glee
We danced to the tent, and inside they went
Leaving behind poor little old me.

From there I went home, in the dark, all alone
And I smiled though no one could see
I'd touched a strange person, been infected for certain
The strange one, from now, would be me!

Colour

Awash with colour, I've more to say
An opal blue on a field of grey
The red of anger leading me astray
Awash with colour, in fear I lay.
Awash with colour, is it the green of leaf?
Or the green of jealousy, good grief
How am I to know? It beggars belief
Awash with colour, let only angels speak.
Awash in colour, I've no more to say
Opal fades back into mundane grey.

One Day in June

My story starts one cold October
I was close to home but far from sober
The night she came and took me over
She arrived one day in June.

Just one month after I was twenty-one
My life was jaded but just begun
When she became my earth and sun
She arrived one day in June.

She arrived one day, one cold chilly day
She arrived one day in June
My destiny found me
Now it's love that surrounds me
And I blame it all on one day in June.

There's No Time

Well, my friends, there is no time
Today has come and I have no rhyme
I had planned a piece that was so sublime
But now we're here and there's no time.

There's no time to speak of empathy
Of the past that was or what could be
Or the rights of all to equality
It would be nice but there's no time.

There's no time to speak of animal rights
Just ship them off and out of sight
It took TV to see the light
It was cruel but there's no time.

And there are so many things I would say
Like how marriage is great unless you're gay
How the demands of a few get into the way
It's not fair but there's no time.

And I would like to speak on the hand we've dealt,
On climate change and polar melt
On the harvest of krill and the dying of kelp
But I fear that there's no time.

Yet I'd mention religion with a hint of disgust
And I'd finish with dogma like 'in god we trust'
So I could fall to my knees while our fields turn to dust
It sounds easy 'cause there's no time.

There's no time like now is all I can say
We can't close our eyes and just wish it away
Or let personal demons ever hold sway
'Cause there's no time like now, there's no time like today.

The Dance

I may be scared, I may be crazy
And truth be told, I'm way too lazy
My soul may be sold, 'cause I feel so cold
Yet I still do the dance.

I once was young, different from now
Thought my song was sung, yet someone called it foul
It got all too hard, I got trapped in bars
Yet I still did the dance.

Then I met…now a memory
My stage had been set, almost destiny
A bitter lie, still I will not cry
But I'll still do the dance.

I will pretend, that I'm still a part
Until the end, my merry lark
In the wind I'll bend, call myself a friend
So I can do the dance.

And yet, when the time has come
I'll fight to the death, and if the bastard won
I will contest, I tried to do my best
When I did the dance.

Web Attack

The internet… What a grand design
You can shop from home if you're so inclined
I tried once because I was slack
One button pressed and web attack!

Did I want to insure my life?
Pets and children… Even wife?
House and contents… Add the car
Special rates if you don't go far.
Would I like a better deal
On implants I would barely feel?
Liposuction and stomach band
I could look fantastic… Given a hand
A bottom tuck and booby lift
At half the price, almost a gift
And how about dinner for two?
Got no one? Oh, woe be you!
Want someone? We can help with that…

I unplugged myself from my web attack.

Inspiration

Inspiration… Oh damnation, where did inspiration go? I
Saw each phrase, each
Turn of page but now I'll never know
I've sat in front of this flickering screen, the
Laughing blank page was almost obscene
Lacklustre, quite
Boring and
Easily too clean, where did
Lying inspiration go?
I've re-
Enacted my steps for
Virtually miles
Even looked for meaning
In some strangers smiles
Niggled
Myself into perilous trials
Yet still the words won't flow
Mother of inspiration don't
Undo your grand creation
Save this slave of slippery rhyme
Ever the master of words that aren't mine.

Hair

I've never grown my hair,
Where?
Beneath my shoulder height
I've tried it in so many ways but it never felt quite right
It's only when I shave my head that I finally feel the light
So I never wear my hair,
Where?
Beneath my shoulder height.

There was Sampson and Delilah and even though his hair was long
He was involved too deep in politics
And his choice in girls was wrong
He committed religious suicide all the while singing a song
So I never wear my hair,
Where?
There, 'cause that's too long.

Now I used to be a horse rider
But hair got in my way
It got tangled in the mane and in the tail and in the hay
It even got into my throat when I had fuck all else to say
So I never wear my hair,
Where?
There, but that's OK.

I envied Lady Godiva, naked there upon her horse
If it wasn't for her hair there would have been cause for divorce
Her hair was well below her waist but her modesty was forced
But her husband didn't care
Because his attentions were outsourced.

So I've never grown my hair,
Where?
Just beneath my arse
It always gets too tangled so I think on this I'll pass
Birds could try to nest in it, life would become a farce
So I've never worn my hair,
Where?
Just beneath my arse.

Rapunzel was high up in her tower with her hair just flowing down
The compulsive little hairy freak grew it right down to the ground
People got lost into it… Never to be found
So I've never worn my hair,
Where?
Right down to the ground.

This is the end of my silly tale but if you want more you should look
There's all sorts of silly stories about hair in many books
There's only one thing more I'll say and I hope that I'm on track
I don't care if you cut your hair; if you're lucky, it grows back.
Where?

Love

Some say love is like a current
In a twisted, turbid sea
Some say that love is peaceful
Some say that love is free
Some say that it's an echo
Of a life shared in the past
Some say that it's forever
Some say it can never last.

If you ask me my opinion
I must say that I don't know
For I have seen love overcome
And I have seen love go
I've seen it make some people strong
Some weakened at the knees
And I've seen it eat some people up
Like a horrible disease.

For me I have to live in hope
For that I can't disguise
And I pray that I will know it
When I look into her eyes
And I hope that she will see it
And that she will feel the same
So we both can have a partner
In life's complicated game.

The Cat in the Window

There was a cat in the window when I woke up this morning
It seemed like an omen, a terrible warning
It was there for a moment just as I woke
Then it disappeared in a grey cloud of smoke.
It's fading; thank the gods that it's fading.

There was a cat in the window yesterday too
I was still half asleep, didn't know what to do
I wanted to follow, to see where it goes
But still it snuck off on its light kitty toes.
It dodged me, though I followed it lost me.

There was a cat in the window the day before last
Its shadowy presence bespoke of the past
It whispered a warning, the worst that I heard
Then it took to the sky like a great fuzzy bird.
I must see…if my meds are faulty

There was a cat in the window the day before that
But it didn't fly; it just fell with a splat
I'd opened the window to let the thing in
But it fell to the ground with a cacophonous din
I'm sorry…I never wanted to hurt thee.

There was a cat in the window last night as well
It dropped into my dreams then dragged me to hell
It tortured my psyche, rent flesh from my bones
So now I can't sleep and I can't be alone
It haunts me…with its cries it taunts me

When the cat in the window comes to me tonight
I will fall to my knees then I'll put up a fight
First I'll beg its forgiveness but then if I fail
I'll beat it back into hell with its own furry tail!

Why Would You Do That?

Some people jump out of a plane
So that they can never feel the same
Whether they land intact or crush their brains
So why would you do that?

Some leave behind a feathered bed
And climb up Everest instead
They'll either make the summit or end up dead
So why would you do that?

So why would you do that I say?
They'd rather burn up than fade away
Instead of watching life they seize the day
So why wouldn't you do that?

Crush

It's just a crush…
A simple little crush
It doesn't have to mean that much
It's just a look, a glancing touch
My heartbeat skips then starts to rush
My legs get weak and turn to mush
My mundane thoughts turn into lush
Heat starts to flow and so I blush
But it doesn't mean that much
It's just a crush…

The Route to the Rout

(spoken with a slight Scottish accent)

We had come to fight for our lord's right
To tax another's land
'Twas more than this but this beggars bliss
Had us heed only our command.

It was when might was right, there was dark and light
And nothing in between
We ate scraps when able from our lord's table
And we forgot the souls we'd been.

We were on route to the fight, our spirits were bright
Our stomachs were full so we sung
We did great deeds of good, like the honour bound should
And the wretched among us we hung.

Towns opened before us, they gave us their daughters
There were those amongst who forgot
In the most righteous of purges, those who gave in to their urges
Were killed as were those they begot.

There were whispers of doubt but those sounds were drowned out
By the yell of our sweet battle cry
Because over those hills were blaspheming infidels
And we would triumph or all us would die.

So we raged to the rout, those before us died out
We condemned all our souls in the end
For as the blood lust wore oo't all those dead on the route
Were the same souls we'd sworn to defend.

We were the third of crusaders, now no one would aid us
Those who could, would still try to stand
Through disease or through blight, we thought we knew what was right
But we died by our lord's mortal hand.

The Tale of an Old Pair of Boots

These old boots they tell of a weary life
Of miles walked, of strain, of strife
These boots we know should have been replaced
All covered with dirt and flecks of paint
Tread worn out, they had been resoled
The stitches somehow crude and bold
The leather worn and the laces frayed
But it hadn't always been that way

They were the finest of leather, Italian-made
Stronger than silk and softer than suede
The best of the best, the best you could get
And they'd lived the life of a pampered pet
Stuffed up with paper to hold up their shape
Never a scuff, a scratch or a scrape
Kept in the darkness, the colour unfaded
It wasn't too long till they were outdated

Bundled away to a second-hand store
Bought by a guy who worked for the poor
Slowly but surely the boots got worn in
The leather got scraped, the soles became thin
Polished with care, the scrapes nearly gone
The old tread worn out, new tread glued on
Hand-stitched together to see 'em through strife
Their story now told for such is a boot's life.

www.ingramcontent.com/pod-product-compliance
Lightning Source LLC
Chambersburg PA
CBHW062143100526
44589CB00014B/1672